SELF-DISCIPLINE:

Learn How To Build Self-Discipline And Achieve All Your Set Goals

TABLE OF CONTENTS

Introduction

Self-discipline is defined as the ability to stay on the straight and narrow, to hold on to one piece of goal regardless of the temptations and distractions that surround you. It is the ability of an individual to overcome obvious weaknesses, to stay above casual responses to impulse or environmental influence.

An individual with good self-discipline is able to stay above his feelings, make decisions based on rational analysis instead of emotions. Self-discipline is a favorite subject in terms of achieving fast success or accomplishing different goals in a small amount of time. It is a personality trait needed by all but possessed by few. It is a skill that can be learned with consistent practice and dedication. Even learning self-discipline demands some amount of self-discipline.

One of the keyword often missing when discipline comes to the picture is willpower. This is the ability to control the present and the future by creating a power flow around all your dealings. It is ultimately the key to life and the determinant of fate. Without the proper amount of willpower you will be spending every dime you make without proper planning. Willpower is what makes eating good food possible, doing exercises and even taking a step towards developing good relationship.

Willpower goes against the wind of emotions; it helps you do things for their actual benefits instead of resorting to how you feel for the final results of your actions. Procrastination has no place to stay on the mind of a person with a strong willpower. Good social behavior or abstaining from drugs and alcohol regardless of their tempting benefits, making a decision to pursue only healthy activities, begins with the conception of willpower.

Although scientists have argued about discipline to be the product of circumstances, recent studies have shown that self-disciplined individuals exercise the same control over situations regardless the pressure they are faced with. The acclaimed model of self-control is the source of willpower that acts like a muscle, which demands a lot of flexibility and exercises to keep it fit for future troubles.

It also has limitations, whereby lapses may occur from time to time. This is natural especially among individuals with healthy personalities, when faced with several or simultaneous series of challenging situations, almost causing brain fatigue, making us ignore rational judgment, to allow the emotions to take over our impulses.

In the case of excessive exertion of the energy needed to exercise self-discipline, self-control may be limited even in the most morally equipped individuals. Fortunately, a study published in the Journal of Brain Physiology showed that the power needed to exercise discipline can be replenished. Human beings can easily fuel their willpowers to stay longer enduring different and even simultaneous setbacks, and still remain on the straight and narrow. For example, the simple sugar and carbohydrate intake can increase the brain's willpower by 130 percent.

The food we eat has a great impact on the amount of willpower we have as people, but still, self-control can only be achieved through constant physical practices. The more you exercise self-control in your daily dealings, the better you do. According to another research at the Northwestern University, the simple act of self-control has a significant effect on the level of blood glucose. Ultimately, self-control lowers the level of blood glucose. Another side of the same study discovers that self-control or discipline can be attained when sugar is consumed.

Another mechanism that restores self-control is motivation. The dopamine system in the brain responds to signals and sensations of rewards and sweetness. When the brain is alerted that a certain possibility of reward is on the way, it pushes the impulse towards creating an action that will make the reward come even faster. So motivation is achieved when an energy boost is being sensed. Physically, the individual will make more effort despite the rational reasons why he needs to stop or even give up.

Cognitive and physical persistence are also important in building the self-discipline muscles. Learning and productivity are determined by the level of such disciplines.

Skills of Self-Discipline

Resisting temptations and actually finishing a task at the appointed time requires actual skills instead of a mere decision. The skills of self-discipline are elemental and must be considered one after the other for one to understand the essence of taking a progressive step to develop this attribute. The most important need for self-discipline in adults and kids is the cultivation of functional independence.

People with self-discipline learn things faster than normal people and they apply the knowledge accumulated due time, even consistently. Authority is often found at the born of this model of self-discipline and the people you once depended on might be surprised by your sudden breakout. These four models include commitment, consistency, completion and concentration.

Both act significantly in bringing self-discipline into the light. Evidently, one model cannot do without the other. They are both supportive in providing a proper self-actualization in kids and providing a definitive model of decision making in adults. The level of acumen which might be important for solving complex problems is often determined by the level of concentration an individual is able to put on a certain activity or detail that will help in finding answers. On the other hand, looking at problem from several angles is important in assessing all the images, and seeing beyond what others see, without the need to rush unto creating solutions just to get out of the situation.

Enemies of self-discipline are easily targeted and eliminated using the four models altogether. The higher understanding achieved in studying this models, the better a person does in achieving functional independence. Leadership skills are initiated through the perfection of the elements, because people will practically look up to you for a solution. As your intelligence level increase by actually solving a problem, the level of cognitive control also increases.

Commitment

Commitment is the ability to deliver an individual service and substance unto something as promised through legal agreement or empathy. This is another form of loyalty that renders an individual selfless to be able to fulfill a promise without the need to be pushed or forced. Some people have weak commitment count even in the case of doing by their own words; while others do well in committing to task without compromise for a longer period of time.

Committed individuals are reliable and often given responsibilities and chances for leadership. The main quality that organizations value in committed individuals is the ability to finish things. They are trustworthy and practically diligent in getting things done. Due to the fact they believe they could do as promised, people also believe in them.

Self-doubt is further eliminated to give chance for a sound environment to have a working acumen towards problem solving and creativity. The challenges faced when practicing these skills most of the time is procrastination. This brings about delay and even avoidance in fulfilling said promises or following through with a given plan.

Most people use the power of the emotions to stay committed to a particular task. For example, people with high emotional intelligence align their emotions to the rewards after fulfilling a promise, something that will bring about emotional satisfaction; this will automatically become their motivation to stay even longer on a particular task. The normal person sees this attribute and calls it self-discipline.

Consistency

Consistency is the engine for every successful pursuit of dreams and goals. Starting from learning process to the implementation of knowledge or skills, the most important part of the puzzle is whether you are consistent or not. Even in terms of commitment, people only trust your promises when they acknowledge that you are consistent with your words and action plans. The only people who get things done are the ones who understand the concept of consistency. It brings about persistence, which conquers all barriers and challenges in relationship and business.

The continual effort that is required to maintain an effect is very important to the development of a disciplined personality. Sometimes consistency means repeating the same thing over and over again, therefore becoming perfect. Finishing things before a deadline becomes only possible when consistency is applied.

So, consistency becomes the root of self-discipline and a stem for growth in different aspect of life. Also, habits can be easily cultivated using the concept of consistency. Even the hardest but positive habits can be cultivated in a short amount of time. Becoming productive is a habit that most entrepreneurs cultivated and working relentlessly toward permeating this habit in their employees and team members.

The consistent has tolerance for boredom and sets to conquer any daunting effect of a normal work process. Most people need motivation to stay above boredom, but a consistent person acknowledges the presence of boredom; welcomes it and still continue the one thing that matters to his work process. Because irregular application renders a work process ineffective and in business, losses might occur.

Consistency can be attained by first focusing on simple tasks; making plans to achieve them regardless of the circumstances or the emotions at the moment. A person should be able make daily plans and at a definite time and be able to follow through. You should include repetition as part of your learning process until perfection is attained. The perfection of a work done is one of the primary motivations of consistency, which makes the individual focused only on the results instead of the boring work process.

Completion

This is related to consistency but this in particular focuses on getting things done regardless of the method used. Some people resort to finishing tasks by involving as many people as possible in the work process. They don't need to consistently go over the output of the work because they believe in the abilities of their employees. But the unique thing about individuals having the completion skill is the ability to follow through regardless how hard things get.

They operate both in favorable and unfavorable environments and a particular situation does not change the mode of their work process, instead they push even harder in order to remain strong and unfathomed. This people are persistence even when faced with bad experiences, emotional breakdown, frustration and fatigue. They take into consideration the benefit of a work process instead of the actual strains and challenges involved.

Although completion and persistence are argued by psychologists to be determined by the energy in the particular goal, it also depends on the experience of that particular person in using these skills to achieve his or her goals. So completion is also a skill to be learned and perfected in every work process.

Unfortunately most people have low tolerance to unfavorable work process especially when they have tried several times and failed. So they give up easily and never get back on the horse for a reasonable amount of time. There is always a chance you will give-up when you run out of determination regardless of your intensions on the initial part of the plan. The best way to perfect this skill in your daily life is by practicing completion every day.

Simply, instead of focusing on how hectic the work will be, focus on the rewards that await you once you finish the job. Also, always set a deadline in order to stretch your ability to finish tasks faster every day. Do not leave a given task unfinished; always have the zeal to finish before you stop, regardless of the strain.

One suggestion made by the business psychologist Zuma Bingham, is to break your task into smaller pieces, so you can have a clear picture on what is to be done at a particular time. By dissecting your tasks into smaller pieces, you will be able to manage them without stress as every step will be accounted as a progress.

Concentration

Distraction is the opposite of concentration often experienced by almost every normal human being in the 21st century. Only few are able to resist the power of distraction and actually avoid getting stuck in irrelevant activities. Also, concentration determines the amount of time a person can finish a task, which practically gives a clear difference in the productivity of an employee even in the work place.

The efficiency of a work done is also determined by the amount of concentration given to the process and for how long. One of the determinants of concentration is the speed of a work process. On the other hand, speed also helps an individual as to practice concentration, becoming perfect in paying attention.

Entertainment and other media distractions are the strongest sources of distractions not only in young people but also in adults. These frequent interruptions keep people stuck in a single work process over a long period of time. Progress is stunted and the ability to move past one stage of life to another becomes challenging and almost impossible.

The art of concentration demands that individuals should concentrate on what they can do best, instead of settling for a challenge. When you practice concentration on familiar tasks, it will be easier to practice the same skill on unfamiliar tasks. You should turn every activity into a game that requires winning. Regardless of the situation, always make time for passion.

Even better, pursue your passion, and make sure that you accumulate enough information to keep your brain stimulated by every progressive step you take. Focus your attention on one task at a time. Do not set different goals and expect to multitask just to achieve everything. As you increase the time spent on a single task, also reduce the number of task you are required to carry out at a definite time.

Self-Discipline and Accomplishment (Importance of Self-Discipline)

Self-discipline is neither harsh nor restrictive. It is about finding balance in a particular work process and to still be able to get things done. The essence of self-discipline is to have an exclusive quality of life, where everything will happen at the appointed time with faith and belief for relevant outcome. There are no limitations in the activities you can involve in for fun.

You don't have to stop giving attention to the people that matter in order to attain a significant level of self-discipline. Your efficiency depends on the time balance you can create and following through with all your schedules, either personal or business. Your inner strength should manifest in showing self-control even as you have the fun of your life. The aim is to be in control of every situation at hand, and make sure you win every fight using logics instead of aggressiveness or literal fight.

Be fast in making decisions and slow in changing them. Never underestimate the power of simple distraction. Exercising your power over every effort and disposition helps in developing simple practices that will elevate you to the top. Perseverance and speed, which are very important in achieving any significant goal, should be applied. Having the proper amount of self-discipline gives the ability to overcome laziness, procrastination and even addictions. It is the essence of control over the things that go out and comes into your life.

Instant gratification can be easily rejected and an individual may not succumb to pleasure instead of saving his strength for something bigger, more significant to life goals. This person may resort to putting effort and time in achieving his goals and dreams instead of using the shortcut which might only lead to a short-term success and then regrets.

What self-discipline does?

Greater problem solving skills

The perseverance and persistence obtained when practicing self-discipline renders the person capable of managing problems and conquering challenges. This person will not be afraid to be exposed to challenges, thus he becomes familiar with certain types of problems, and how to solve them. He rises above emotions and aim for the solution without the emotional impact the problem might cause.

This person has understood the concept of focus, and can apply self-discipline even in solving problems that may not have to do with them or their personal interests. They intentionally create a circumstance that will impose pressure, so they can experiment with the skills they have for problem solving. People often contact them for advice or mediation.

Great self-esteem and self-confidence

A finisher has a reason to be confident of his achievements and his actions toward achieving a given goal. Discipline is all about getting things done. Less and less people are able to get things done these days, so the finisher knows that he is always a step above other people.

Individuals with good self-discipline also have greater self-esteem as they actualize the value of time spent on tasks or people wisely. They are always conscious of time and what they do, and value themselves very much in a work process. They expect to be treated with respect and do not accept less, only more.

Avoiding failure and recovering from defeat

Self-discipline can ultimately help you avoid unnecessary failures. Part of being discipline is having a greater focus and understanding of your surrounding and tasks, so you tend to become more aware of all the forces around your work process. You are a finisher, so maybe you had experience with a similar person or task. You take the correct step to avoid the repetition of mistakes, so you become ultimately perfect in reaching your goals.

Relationship and health will be maintained without the need for relapses or compromise. The self-control is very important in relating with people and achieving a long lasting relationship. You will be able to secure only friends that value your time and company. In business, you can easily focus on relating with people that will help in your elevation to the next level.

Since your consistency is also stimulated, your products or services remain alive even as you partner with other people that will help your work done. Obesity and other impulsive problems are avoided.

Overcoming disorders and addictions

Lack of self-discipline can bring about negative habits. When you lack control of your friends or the things you do on a daily basis, you easily succumb to addictions such as drinking, smoking and even drug addiction. In a research published by the Journal of Addiction and Substance Abuse, eating disorder is associated with lack of self-discipline just like any other form of addiction.

Individuals who lack actual control of their impulses tend to be vulnerable to negative habits. The essence of discipline which include spiritual growth, self-improvement, skill development and keeping physically fit becomes absent in the lives of addicts.

Core Principles of Time Management

Time management is about productivity. People with extreme time management skill tend to be self-disciplined and focused. They are high achievers and have maximum productivity count towards each and every project.

They have understood the core principles of time management so well and are applying every bit of detail on relevant daily activities. They have understood that time management is a fundamental skill that one needs to keep learning in order to become disciplined.

Motivation vs. time management

The time you spend on particular task directly affects your motivations. Time management demands a great deal of motivation, even at the beginning of a work process. You need to find your actual motivation, which may involve the reason you want to embark on a particular journey and your life's purpose.

Let your motivation be permanent and valid regardless of the emotions you are going through at a particular period of time. Let the goal you have at hand be a driving force to infuse consistency and persistence even when you don't feel like doing anything. Allow yourself to float. Feel everything; the disappointment, the fear, the failure and the annoyance, and still continue the journey anyway.

Every shortcoming should be seen as an opportunity for growth and improvement. Practically, focus on the lessons to be learned, the faults and all other factors that may help you avoid failure next time you try the same thing.

Instead of starting over immediately, take a break in order to reflect and then come back with full energy on your goals. The aim here is to make sure your productivity is increasing a day at a time. Keep track of this progress to become even more motivated as you seek improvement.

The timeout principle

Relate with other people, take a break from all work or business contacts and connect with people you can just talk about casuals things with. Do not resort to lonely breaks or weekends. Go out and socialize, in order to get a better mental balance. Let your relationship with the kids, spouse, parents and friends count. Allow time for the people that love you for who you are; the people who will stand by you even when everything is falling apart.

Do not take your personal relationship for granted. Most people make the mistake of avoiding or disregarding the important people for the excuse of having limited time to interact or play together. But once the relationships are nurtured and are cultivated in good faith, your mood about a work process or business will change course, thus expanding your acumen as you pursue even bigger goals.

Speaking on phone may not be enough for stimulating real intimacy between partners. Thus your mind needs to be in the moment by actually being in the moment physically with your loved one. Remember, self-discipline is not just about persisting on achieving physical goals, it is also about achieving emotional satisfaction; to make sure you commit moderately in making people that look up to you feel loved and appreciated.

Also, understanding their needs and actively acting towards providing those needs is very important. This accounts to the development of habit towards a substantial self-discipline.

Business vs. time management

Time management in business cannot be overemphasized. Making that call at the definite time and finishing the work of a client at the promised time determines whether your reputation will remain the same or not. Losing a job and finding one reflects on your time management skills.

This skill reduces mistakes and unfavorable argument between business partners or disagreements due to clash of events or programs. The business atmosphere of the 21st century is getting sophisticated every day and you are demanded to blend with the sophistication. This means that your time management skills must be exclusively sophisticated.

With time management, you will make sure you don't miss opportunities by meeting your deadlines and actually starting a new deal at the appointed. Finishing fast, which is also an attribute of the self-disciplined, is very important in business, which can only be attained with proper time management. The opportunities in business are tremendous once you apply this principle of time management as you increase the quality of your work

One way to acknowledge the progress of your work due time is to dissect your goals into smaller pieces and appoint time for them individually. This way you don't need to rush a work process because you consciously know that you can finish this part of the job at the appointed time.

Also, you will achieve self-confidence in your business approach, which is a very important quality to secure quality clients, which means more money. On the side of self-discipline, you are indirectly building your ability to stay longer on a task and using the tight amount of concentration without stressing yourself about the outcome because you know it must be great.

Lastly, let your body respond positively to the task or stress you are exposed to, when running a business. Leave business at the workplace and come back home like a normal person. Do not bring your office work to the bedroom especially when it can become a habit. Instead, make a plan to actually finish everything while in the office. Using good time management and self-discipline, you will be surprised how much work you will get done in the few hours you spend in the office.

Efficiency vs. effectiveness

Efficiency showcases your capacity of performance and effectiveness tells whether your work is going to serve the proposed need. In business and personal relationship, you should first focus on effectiveness, then the efficiency of your work process in achieving the effectiveness in particular. Regardless of the energy you spend or the hours spent to get things done, only the result determines its value.

So, let your commitment matter, but do not allow the need for work to block your judgment. Feel the need to be effective in all endeavors, stay away from the neutral ways of finishing task. Do not settle for less, always go for something bigger than what you have and plan to be effective in all ways. Make time for evaluation during a work process to make sure that you are still going towards the right direction.

Also, focus on the importance and try to spend less time on things that don't matter regardless how you love to do them. Stay away from things that may add just a little value to your business or personal life. Always do more when you know that value can be found in a particular work process.

Avoid multitasking in order to direct your creative energy on a single task until it is finished. Principle of time management demands that individuals should pursue a discovered value with full energy at the time of discovery, thus you can benefit from the fruit of your labor while the soil is still fertile.

This despises the concept of extreme planning; therefore hastiness is required for maximum profit, regardless of the perceived risk. Also, you should consider the resources available and for how long you will have a particular access to such resources.

So, you should never run out of stuck, and your input must be as effective and efficient as possible. Do not ignore the importance of resting in-between tasks to reenergize. This is the simplest forms of finding effectiveness during a work process that require insight. Thus you will be able to finish more work and also with the effectiveness you desire.

The aim is to avoid both physical and mental stress. Only with a sound mind will you recognize and develop ideas for a significant breakthrough. Relieving stress on the other hand also provides such amount of effectiveness. Music and physical exercises help a lot in relieving mental and physical stress.

The hierarchy of needs

Focus on your hierarchy of needs and only focus on things you will need now. Take care of your current needs before jumping into wants and fantasies. Make sure that you are living comfortably without a single debt before thinking about the expensive vacation or outing.

Make sure you wear good clothes and feel comfortable interacting with people before you resort to other expensive activities. Always eat healthy before pursuing a task. Your productivity in a meeting or work is affected by the kind of food you consume; either you've had breakfast or not. Your focus will be affected by your gut movements. Taking care of your primary needs cannot be overemphasized in achieving good time management and in turn becoming well balanced in your quest for self-discipline.

Also do not ignore your emotional needs which include the need for social safety, healthy self-esteem, friends and family support, love, self-worth and the need to feel appreciated. All these are mostly ignored by people; by which reduces their motivation and drive towards betterment especially when pursuing something big.

Let your interpersonal relationship grow to the utmost without losing a personal touch to your goals and dreams. The aim is to maintain a mental and emotional wellbeing and to also develop some amount of emotional intelligence in the process of goal pursuit. You should be able to set your priorities right and never compromise except when you are left with no choice.

This is where you begin setting a particular standard of living, where you will have extreme control over the things that come and go in your life. Let go of dreams that can't be reached, give no time for mediocrity and just focus on what know how to do best in order to ensure victory. Fully assess yourself and make plans on the things you want to spend time on, the most important, the average and the less important. Put everything in their rightful positions and begin working on the necessary elements one day at a time.

Building Willpower and Discipline in Students

According to a research at the University of Pennsylvania, performance of students cannot be exclusively determined by their level of IQ but by the amount of self-discipline applied over a particular semester or toward studying a particular course. Ultimately, a student's intellectual potential is determined by the level of self-discipline being exercised over a particular period of time.

The researchers went as far as performing experiments on students by predicting their academic performances based on their default self-discipline count. Roughly, the result checked even though academic variances have to occur due to the differences in approach and sometimes, luck. The final GPA although matched the predicted data, which as a result confirmed the essence of self-discipline both among students and adults in determining a successful future result.

Leveraging the imagination

The imagination is a powerful tool for both creation and the infusion of feelings. Creative visualization is recommended according to the research as the imaginative tool for exercising the brain muscles. This brings about some kind of lubrication through which the brain will remain fit and withstand stress even in the case of long work hours.

This brain work out must also involve relaxation in order to allow for reflection and proper build up. Do not stress yourself too much during this exercise, you should start slow and build yourself to stiffness. The visualization and rest exercises are also great for building your willpower. This is important in eliminating all elements of temptations and distractions or to be in the midst of temptations and still thrive, getting things done like you have power over everything.

Develop soft skills

As a student, the incentives of high performance are usually the scores on the report cards. These scores may mean nothing in the office or when dealing with business associates or partners. So in order to widen the balance a student has for self-discipline, soft skills must be introduced earlier.

These skills include learning how to communicate to certain type of people, expressing oneself without the need to hide behind flaws, and being able to speak in the crowd without being anxious. Communication skills should be backed by leadership skills, by which students who develop these skills at an early age tend to be flamboyant and extremely disciplined about their studies and skills development.

When you feel like a leader, you always want to be ahead of other people, thus self-discipline will be unconsciously applied during the process of study or even during school games. Learning about teamwork is also very important among students in order to provide for motivations that will sustain the mission for self-discipline.

Teamwork is easily applied among students although some students still prefer doing everything alone. Such students need to learn how to associate with other students to gain support systems and also to become a support for someone's self-discipline. Ultimately, you become better in everything you do when someone else is trying to do the same thing and you resort to helping each other.

Also, students should learn about profit and loss. Even when you are not a business student, understanding the concept of profit and loss will help you in developing the right financial mindset; to make decisions that will stick, and to make sure that you derive motivation from the knowledge.

Last but not the least; students must be exposed to emotional intelligence. It is important in every learning process that a person develops a control over the emotions and be able to differentiate between intellectual and emotional decisions. A student should be able to relate with the emotions of other students, to provide for empathy and even sympathy, in order to connect with other people.

Also, emotional intelligence becomes very important in honing the emotions during studies and lectures. Not allowing the emotions to take control of your dispositions, you can be able to develop a willpower that will help you build self-discipline easily.

Building resiliency

Resiliency is important not just in building self-discipline but in developing positive habits about goals in general. One way to build resiliency as a student is by pairing with other students. This is to have a constant reminder of your progress and to be aware of your shortcomings, to be alerted whenever you are about to deviate from your said objectives. Resiliency is about standards, and people that are concern about us must be also concerned about the standards we suppose to maintain.

This people should know whether you are lying about a progress or exaggerating about a process. In no time you will discover the essence of building self-discipline by being monitored.

When you hate it

Another definition of self-discipline is the ability to do something even when you don't have extreme love for it. Among students, self-discipline is the ability to do something even when you completely hate it and the people that are involved. This routine should be followed consistently to avoid emotional relapse.

Exclusively make a list of the activities you hate starting from the most important ones to the less important. Analyze the benefit of doing those things and rearrange your list based on the things you will achieve after finishing the task. Take a deep breath and begin acting toward that task nonstop.

The aim here is to focus on the lazy side of your personality and to involve in activities that will stimulate finishing things instead of procrastination. This provides for willpower and enhanced self-control, which are very important attributes of a self-disciplined individual.

By involving in such activities you will realize that self-discipline is something to be learned; as you grow to achieve more control, you will realize that your performance both in studies and association with people will improve significantly.

Plan ahead of time

The earlier you plan for something the better chances you will do it. Simply, planning has both physical and mental effects. Physically, you will have scheduled time to actually pursue a goal that has been set. You will have no doubt about the preparatory actions you need to take in order to bring your plans into reality. Mentally, your mind will prepare for the occurrence of this incidence, which in turn reduces the chances of procrastination. It also stimulates interest and the mind will picture the activity to be extremely easy.

As a student, part of this planning is actually reading ahead of time and learning how to solve all the equations even before quiz or exams. When you read ahead of lectures, you automatically develop the zeal to attend the lectures in order to compare what the lecturer will say with your research. As a benefit, you understand the subject matter better and you don't have to stress about focusing extremely on the details any further.

This will create a mental balance where control and willpower will be actualized. According to a research at the New York State University, students that invest more time in planning for a semester tend to have higher self-discipline and consequently perform better than the rest of the students. This planning does not have to be exclusively focused on studies, planning for a class party, field trip, fun project and group lessons also help in building such control.

When a student has a clear plan about the coming week, there is a better chance that free time will be utilized for the best. Even when some lectures are cancelled, something productive can be easily fixed on the timeline. It also reduces the chance of emotional disturbances, making every challenge count as a chance for improvement.

Leverage the working memory

Make your short term memory an engine for self-discipline. Working memories are the short term memories, often used to carry out urgent task. As a student, working memory is important for surprise quiz and other exercises that require instant brain stimulation. This helps in developing self-control over distractions and being able to focus on a task without deviation.

Students should improve their memorization and recall skills by involving in word games and other exercises capable of keeping the brain on point. Doodling is encouraged among higher students for achieving focus during classes; it improves your concentration in the moment and helps you recall the same moment when you put a pen on a paper.

Apart from your jotter or worksheet, always have a piece of paper for doodling. If you are not comfortable with doodling things, take the time to draw things that maybe relevant to the subject matter being discussed in class. Also, in order to improve your recall skill, use repetition of words or the replay of a particular scenario on your head over and over again. Make sure that you actualize the most effective method of developing your working memory.

The brain break technique

Take a timeout from all the planning, studying and listening to lectures. Make time for nothingness, where relaxation and getting wasted are involved. Involve in activities that do not require insight or deep thinking. You don't need to wait until the end of the semester to relax. You need to relax in order to recharge, achieving even better focus.

Use the time in-between tasks to take a nap or stay in a quiet place with less noise. Take some deep breathes in order to refocus your mind before going back to the task. Conventionally, 5 to 10 minutes are enough for proper brain breaks. For example, after 2 hours lectures, you might need to go out and get some air.

Another study at the same New York State University proved that students find composure, self-control and focus when lectures are shortened by short breaks. Further study confirmed that, regardless of the things a lecturer needs to cover, focusing on bullet points and summarizing the topic works better in theoretical students.

Even in terms of arithmetic, purging the brain to withstand long hours of exercises might be suffocating, so normal students are required to take break after at most, 4 hours of arithmetic.

Reward your self-control

Always create a reward system for exercising a certain amount of self-control when carrying out an activity. Self-control helps you achieve focus, so you achieve things even faster and do better in your work process. Always have a treat waiting for you at the end of the task.

Reward yourself a good time; so whenever you feel like giving up or delaying on a task you can remind yourself of what you might be missing for not moving fast. Also, the value of the reward should be actualized based on personal interest and needs, not based on what the society thinks is valuable or not.

How to Be More Resilient When Things Get Tough

The secret of surviving challenging times

At a certain level of life challenges become inevitable and we are expected to thrive regardless of our strengths and flexibilities. Self-discipline cannot thrive when adversity cannot be resisted. A person must be able to win, and continue winning even when everything seems dark and gloomy.

You need to accept change even one day, be the creator of change. You need to able to bend your principles without breaking them. You need to allow yourself to feel all the hurt and challenges; the adversities and the disappointments and continue the journey any ways.

Resilience is a survival skill that must be learned and applied in order to achieve excellence in business, career and relationship. Growth comes from the number of failures and challenges one goes through, but the difference between learning from your mistakes and allowing them to break you is the capacity of resilience you possess.

Coping with mental stress in this case does not depend on your physical or mental capacity, it depends on your zeal and persistence, and the willingness to pick yourself up, dust off and keep on moving when knocked down.

Firstly, you need to believe in yourself and all that you are. You must believe in the effort you are making right now for bigger achievements. You must believe that you are intelligent enough to conquer these challenges, and to start from the beginning, and still come back a winner.

Secondly, you must believe in your bigger goal. You don't need anybody to believe that your ideas or efforts will pay off with something bigger. The only person you need to believe in you is you. Take the time to develop your skills and never stop learning from other successful people. Your faith determines your mode of action; it determines your energy and ultimately the speed of your success.

Resilience is the product of good behavior and constant habits. These behaviors are born of thoughts of greatness and determination for betterment. The actions you take every day toward a particular goal confirms your thought, and in turn provides greater influence to the amount of mental effort you make into manipulating your way to accomplishment

Even the person with the lowest intelligent quotient can thrive among smart people once resilience is developed through intense learning. The challenges that are unfamiliar to people with high intelligence is already common with the average stunner, so he becomes ultimately better at thriving during challenges.

Resilience also helps build your emotional muscle, to shove emotional distractions aside just to continue on your task. People with developed resilience tend to find it easier to apply emotional intelligence in hastening their work process. Because it is the combination of mental and emotional energy, only those who are willing to face real challenges without the need to run away from the responsibility of breaking out, are able to reach a definite level of resilience.

Creation of meaning

Create a sense of purpose for every goal you set to achieve. Do not involve in a work process just because everybody you know is doing the same. Let your sense of purpose fuel your desire for greatness; let that desire be a motivation even in times of trouble. Purpose defines your meaning in your life's endeavor.

The aim is to be able to have a broader perspective of setbacks, so that you won't find a reason to stop just yet. People that easily give up are often not driven by true purpose. Distractions and challenges will have no effect on your motivation or speed inasmuch as your purpose is intact.

Regardless of the complexity of your personal experience, you will not lose concentration. There must be a different definition of your meaning as you set to achieve a particular goal. Write them in a short form and hang them on your wall, to be seen every morning.

Use a quote that reminds you of your purpose as a screen saver on your smart phone or computer. Let your actions and the people you meet remind you of what you don't want to be and exactly what you want to be.

In all these, you must be willing to learn from each and every disappointment you are faced with. Do not ignore your emotions. Listen to your feelings and make sure you feed them properly.

Build relationships

Relationship is the pillar of determination through which any purpose will thrive. Your purpose becomes less valuable when your relationships are shaky. Starting from your personal relationship with family and friends, make sure that you have a strong bond with the people that know and love you for who you are.

Also, in business, build strong relationship with likeminded individuals and never be blinded from the value someone can add to our life. These people will support you directly or indirectly to make sure that you thrive during challenges. Regardless of your level of success, your mental or physical strength, you will always need a human support system.

Be it emotionally, physically or spiritually, never stop connecting to people that matter. Also, try as much as possible to eliminate toxic people from your life. Once you discover that a certain person has negative influence on your goals or dreams make sure you stay away from them. Even if you are dealing with a family member, you cannot disown them, but you can reduce the number of times you have to talk or meet.

Become a giver of hope

Take care of others even as you take good care of yourself. Listen to someone's complaints and challenges, and try to contribute moderately in making their lives easier. Exercising resilience may not be just about getting to know yourself and your strengths; it is also about understanding people and their weaknesses. Once you connect with others at the level of empathy, you will begin to realize your strengths and natural gifts of understanding challenging situations.

Therefore the strength needed to rise up when you get knocked down by life will only be a step away from your grasp. This quality becomes very important to your social image and personal reputation when you are able to care about others even when you are going through a hard time.

People will see you as a model; even the ones you think are strong enough will begin to regard you as the leader, the hero of kindness. Let your selflessness thrive even when everything you can see or feel is reasons not to continue. Once you are able to pass this level of perspicacity, self-discipline will be easier to build.

Pick yourself up

Once again, failure is determined by the decision you make whenever you fall. Your story will be determined by the effort you make to pick yourself up when hit by failure. This should not just be a one-time attitude, rising up should be your habit, a model of living.

Let your lifestyle be all about facing challenges and defeats but never allowing yourself to be actually defeated. Let your zeal to thrive surpass the power of challenges caused by people or a work process.

Stay ready

Stay ready for challenges; stay prepared to solve problems even in the wee hours. Never stop being logical in your endeavors. Train yourself to become even better in handling your business so that the reason for a particular failure can be actualized and dealt with.

Be prepared for negative comments about your innovation. Stay ready for the people who will make an effort to make sure what you are doing is dragged on the ground. Be ready for success, because if you cannot handle success, it may not last.

Make definite plans for the future and remember that your achievement will solely depend on what you planned. Even if your plan looks perfect from the beginning, never stop reaching for more knowledge and evaluation.

Consider criticism from professionals. Assess your plans and your purpose, make sure the changes you will make correspond to the main reason you are chasing this goal. Never deviate from the main purpose. Once you deviate from the initial path, you will automatically lose your grand motivation.

If the aim was to make money, all the new inputs should be focused on creating maximum profit. If the aim was to create a societal change, all the input should be focused on selfless contribution to the community. If the aim was to create personal change, let your endeavors be focused on this change relentlessly.

Always keep your mind on the reward that is awaiting you, and make every effort to make yourself worthy. Work on your self-esteem and self-confidence in order to learn from people while you interact with them. Instead of becoming anxious about your innovation or feeling like you are being judged, focus on people and their body languages. Be prepared to assess your environment and the people, so any decision you make will correspond to their needs, therefore meeting your particular aim.

Keep improving

Realize that you cannot begin the journey today and win today. The challenges and failures you will face are important part of your growth as a person. They are exactly the things that will contribute to your greatness. They shape your personality and build your self-discipline above the average person.

So, even when you make the wrong choices, forgive yourself as you continue to pursue greatness. "The little resilience you have today will grow into something bigger only if you don't stop chasing what makes you better as a person."

Courageousness and braveness is determined by the willingness of heart, to face and to conquer regardless of the method being used. You should focus on the power you have right within, and never allow physical forces to cause negative reaction, especially the one that might wound your effort.

Keep getting tough

Great people are tough and principled. They don't have fear and they take risk without thinking twice. They only focus on possibilities rather than limitations. They adapt easily to new situations and are flexible with their methodologies even when their principles remain intact.

Worst times are expected, but what makes the difference is the resilience applied, through self-discipline and discernment. When they see a tough situation coming at them, they quickly look for leverage in order to aim for defeat. They are humble but proud of the powers they possess in controlling what concerns them. They are soft hearted but tough on their business.

They believe that their endeavors have to be respected, so they set rules for people to follow. When the going gets tough, they become tougher, instead of giving up. They know exactly that physical strength alone cannot bring about success but mental strength, often translated as smartness.

Master the emotions

The importance of emotional intelligence once again cannot be overemphasized in building self-discipline, especially when you are going to use resilience to make this happen. Focus on harnessing positive emotions even in the midst of negativity. Do not allow your emotions to be stimulated by what people do or say, allow yourself to float in your imaginations.

Let your focus be upon the things you want to achieve and how you can reach those goals. Differentiate between positive and negative emotions. Also, differentiate between temporary and permanent feelings. You will come to realization that most negative feelings are temporary. Even the factors responsible for those feelings tend to be temporary.

Use dynamic thinking

Make a distinction between the thoughts and perspectives that created a particular problem and the ones capable of solving the problem. You will realize that the same thoughts that created a problem cannot be used to solve the same problem.

Using static thinking system to solve a problem will only cause more problems, which is mostly interpreted as repeating same mistake over and over again. Firstly, focus on the honesty of your endeavors.

Find out why you failed in the first place and design a logical model to provide for definite solution even as you learn from your mistakes. In the course of problem solving, do not rush the process. Make a deeper analysis of your methods and actualize on the principal causes of your problems before you proceed to the next step.

How to Develop Good Habit

Developing new habit may take up to 3 weeks, but breaking one might take even longer. The most important strategy for breaking bad habit is by replacing it with a good one. If you have a habit of giving up easily instead of persisting until the end, self-discipline is your best guess of habit to replace this weakness.

Stages for developing new habit:

The pre-contemplation stage

On this stage the realization of change in a particular habit is tender. The discovery of problem or weakness through a particular habit may not be recognized easily. Apart from lack of self-discipline, there might be a habit lurking that have cost you a lot in the past.

Even as you begin to realize this bad habit, you don't think changing or switching to a good habit is possible, so you haven't made an effort to create any particular change. On the other hand, people without a clear image of the bad habit they have tend to think their bad habit is a second-nature. They think the faults are default of nature from birth, and see no point in pursuing change. They are not happy and safe but they tend to settle for the less all the time.

The first action to take is to realize when you do things that make you sad or feel bad about yourself. Look into situations that make you feel unsafe and vulnerable; what are your defense mechanisms? Do you have a certain fear that crossing a particular path may cause a disaster to your life in general?

The next step is to cultivate the strength to go through new situations and hope for a change by taking every necessary methodology into consideration. Realize that in order to succeed you will need to try more than once or twice. If you failed once, have it in mind that you are unto something great and once you put more effort, success will become definite.

The contemplation stage

At this stage you have recognized the problem and you are ready to take the necessary step to achieve a reasonable change. You are now honest with yourself and the people around you about the exact weaknesses that are blocking your success. The contemplation is now about how to go about creating this crucial change; whether you believe you can change for good or not; and whether you are ready to take the hard step or not.

At this stage, you might need to avoid overanalyzing your chances for change. You need to start thinking about what to do instead of how your problem is bigger than you. Focus on learning more about the problem and the kind of habit you might be able to apply to create a change that will stick.

Take a moment and visualize the future with you having cultivated the new habit. This will provide a preview of the life you will be living after you take the first step for change. Picture your life in one year or six months from now and you will find the needed motivation.

The preparatory stage

At this stage your decision to cultivate new habit is definite, so it's time to look deep into the details about all the possibilities for change. Also, at this stage you have to believe that you can overcome your bad habit and replace with a good one. You must believe that the action you are going to take toward your problem will change your life, and you are going to do everything to follow through each step. Finally, you must also believe that you will have both physical and mental control over situations, not to be controlled by your habits anymore.

Sketch out the plan on how you want to achieve the change. Do not take a first step toward any change without having a plan. Because in order to stay longer on a project without feeling frustrated, you need to develop a plan. This will also help you as you take the time to develop good self-discipline.

Create a start time for the action plan. Make sure you consider all physical and mental factors in making this plan come to life. Also, consider the energy you have and the need for that action at the particular timeframe.

Adjust your schedule to meet your time plan. In developing new habit, you must assign your action plan to thrive without stress. For your subconscious to truly respond to a new habit, the condition has to be either favorable or rewarding or both. So you should reserve much energy just to make sure the habit comes to life.

Lastly, mark out the benefits of developing the new habit. This should serve as a driving force or motivation whenever you feel like giving up on your dreams and goals. Even when you feel like giving up, a situation relating to one of the benefits will trigger your action plan.

The action stage

Simply, start doing something. It doesn't matter how fast or slow you take this action, just make sure you are moving towards something better than you, something that will make you greater.

The maintenance stage

This is the evaluation stage, where you will go over the changes you have went through over the past few weeks. Make a note of the positive changes, and focus on them. While developing new habits, many things must be involved but make sure you focus on your action plan in order to create the purposed changed.

The termination stage

At this stage, you will realize you don't have any problem with your old habit. The persistent thoughts about going back to old habits have faded away. It is time to relax and enjoy the new habit in order to make it permanent. You need to be in the moment and never allow yourself to be lured away by the thoughts of the benefits of the old habits.

Things you need to understand:

You will not always pass through the stages as stated. You might go as far as stage four and go back to stage two. It is a normal l pattern of change. Contemplation is part of life, so do not beat yourself up when you find yourself contemplating about the value of your actions.

Do not resort to aloneness when pursuing a change in habits. Involve friends, families or guidance to help you stay in the straight and narrow. Most importantly, use your friends as a support system to help you thrive during temptations. The less relapse you experience in the action stage, the faster you will cultivate the new habit.

Reward yourself every time you do something new with the new habit you just cultivated. The self-discipline element of this new habit should be put to use instantly, and the benefit should come in real time. The weight of the step you take doesn't matter as much as the fact that you are actually taking a step.

Learning good habits will take time. You don't have to go as fast as other people. Do not stretch yourself too much in building self-discipline. Allow time for breaks, even as you evaluate your progress with each step you take.

The longer you stay on an action plan, the better. Since you are cultivating a good habit, you should be expecting such habit to become a part of your life. So, do not be afraid to incorporate the habit in your long-term goals. Make it a part of your life as it affects your endeavors and dispositions directly. In this case, you can easily boost your self-efficacy as you get closer to perfection. Let your celebration be about the breakthrough you are creating using the good habit you just developed.

You don't need to take big steps toward a particular change. Since most habit change is about learning something a step at a time, always take your time with each single step you take. Observe the change, go back if you need to, and make sure the purpose of beginning this journey is being met with every step.

Automate the process of your habit change. Again, incorporate the new habit with people and activities that matter the most to you. You don't need to put extra time or energy in cultivating new habits once you are able to attach the action plan with a familiar activity.

Make a commitment strategy to fill up the gap between responsibility and selflessness. Once you feel responsible in achieving a certain task, even when it means developing yourself to the best, you will have more zeal to take the actions necessary for the tasks to come to life.

Overtime, take the time to go back to the reason you are taking the steps. Are you actually making the planned progress? Why do you still need to pursue this change? Is this what you want? How does this change affect me, my friends and my family?

In developing new habit, something must be always removed. Make sure you are not removing something valuable by making a room for the new habit. Make sure you create a balance between doing good and doing well the right way, even to yourself.

Incorporate the SMART goals strategies. Let your goal for creating new habit become specific and measurable. Always be conscious of the value you are getting and how much it affects your life.

How to Deal with Distraction and Achieve Focus

Eliminate all sources of distractions

In your work place or at home, observe your environment and take the necessary steps to remove anything that might cause distractions. A clean office, free of clutter might be a good place to begin. Sometimes you don't eliminate distractions, you stay away from them.

Whatever the case might be, just make sure you stay above them as you intensify your focus on the things that matter to you. Whenever you feel like you are losing focus, take note of new things happening in the environment and determine on the things that are affecting you as a person.

Plan for relaxed work process

You don't need to spend all day working before you can achieve a reasonable amount of success. Just as stated in previous chapters, focus on effectiveness rather than the amount of time you put into work. Take breaks between tasks and make sure you are not stressing yourself by involving in a new task.

Let your self-discipline be actually regulated by the effectiveness of the work done, not the hours spent on a particular project. Work with insights instead of actual blueprint. Always use creativity to get things done, as you involve in activities that will keep your brain balanced and alert.

Take breaks between tasks

Take at least5minutes break to breathe in-between tasks. Never estimate the power of such short breaks. During this break period, allow your mind to roam freely. Keep away from critical thinking by relaxing your body during the process.

During this break period you can also talk to friends or acquaintances. You may also use the time to call your significant other. Just take some minutes off the intense work process in order to recharge your focus momentum.

Find a reason for the particular task

Let interest be consciously acknowledged when pursuing a particular task. Allow yourself to be motivated by a certain part of the work process. Sometimes looking at the big picture is not enough to keep you focused on the straight and narrow. You need to develop a genuine interest in the work process in order to achieve momentary focus. Maybe you like the way you do things differently, or you like the instant output of your work; focus on reaching that definition in order to make sure your focus is purged.

Go visual

Many creative individuals are visual creatures. They tend to be affected by visuals more than mere words. In order to experiment on visual reminders, put up a picture of something that reminds you of your bigger goal on the wall in the office. Observe your feelings and motivations whenever you glance at that picture, especially during a particular work process.

This picture should remind you of why you should work hard and fast, in order to meet the deadline. It should also remind you of the opportunities that might be missed if you don't focus on the work and reach the finish line.

Make use of caffeine

Regardless of the argument about the harm caffeine has on the creative mind, the substance have helped goal-getters of the 21st century in achieving bigger goals in a very short time range. Caffeine makes you feel alert and alive to perform the same tasks for several hours.

Taking a cup of coffee may determine the differences between you finishing a work and allowing yourself to delay your success. Coffee and must chewing gums contain the right amount of caffeine to keep you alert. Do not take coffee to take care of hunger, always focus on its effects and only take it when you need to be alert.

Make use of headphones

Headphones are very important to keep away from the distractions in the modern world. This works perfectly when you want to brainstorm about a problem or creative block and you need to do it right at the moment. Conventionally, wearing headphones means you cannot hear anyone, so no one should make an effort to talk to you.

Even if you are not listening to music, wearing headphones will keep you a step ahead mentally. It is also an indication of focus, to give signal to people that you don't want to chat at the moment.

Use the reward system

The reward system works in developing self-discipline, achieving focus and even creating fast link between success and work. Always allow yourself to anticipate something great whenever you finish a portion of your project. This reward should be viable and motivational.

It should get your blood rushing, increasing your heartbeat and making you go hard on a particular goal. Before you know it, going hard will become a habit and you will be expecting something great even when immediate gratifications are absent.

Use apps

Use applications to block websites that become a source of distraction to you. Stop any notification from "FACEBOOK", "TWITTER" or "INSTAGRAM". Only allow email notifications in order not to miss urgent emails. Use reminder apps to keep you up to date with the things you supposed to be doing at a particular time.

When using the computer, exit every window that is not relevant to your work at the moment. Always keep track of time you spend on the internet and the things you are actually achieving. There are apps that keep the track of time you spend on a website.

Work offline

Turn off your network and work offline. Even if your work involves researches, complete the research part, save all the data and go offline. This is to avoid distractions from social networks, emails or game apps. Also, during an intense work process, turn off your cellphones to make sure you don't get distracted.

Also, instead of constantly using the computer screen, use the old-fashioned paper to jot down ideas during a brainstorming exercise. Have a definite time for checking emails. Check your email at least twice a day, in the morning and evening. Always create a deadline or limit on the amount of time you are to spend on social media every day.

Try meditation

Meditation has long ago proved by scientists to enhance the brain's focus. The exercise of meditating helps putting one's attention in one place. When such exercises are practiced and perfected, intense focus will be easily achieved.

This involves the kind of focus where you won't recognize the things happening in the environment inasmuch as they are not directly affecting you as a person. Practice meditation once a day in order to achieve such amount of focus.

Do not skip your breakfast

Never ever skip your breakfast. And when having breakfast, consider consuming more protein and less starch or carbohydrate. The kind of food you eat will have direct effect to your gut movement and consequently the amount of focus you can achieve.

Also, avoid coffee for breakfast. Caffeine can be used to enhance your concentration in the afternoon, but you don't need it once you have a good protein breakfast. According to a recent research at the Kentucky University, a bowl of oatmeal is enough to increase metabolism, which ultimately leads to greater focus during a particular task.

Students were chosen to take different kinds of breakfast based on personal choices. Students that consumed oatmeal where found to have higher concentration both in class and during quiz.

Make a plan to be focused

Your focus is always affected by the plans you make. The method you choose in handling a particular task reflect deeply on the amount of focus you achieve. If you plan to multitask, you will find it hard to achieve peace that will render your mind relaxed and focused on a particular task.

Plan to achieve one thing at a time, without the need to distract yourself by other responsibilities. Everything is important, but you should plan to spend a considerable amount of time on a particular task without the need to ignore other responsibilities.

Whenever you lose focus...

Whenever you lose focus, try and pinpoint the actual problem. Maybe it's your relationship with people; your family; friends or the people you are doing business with. If people make you lose focus by stimulating your mental or emotional balance, try not to keep in touch with them during a creative task. If the problem is your addiction to a certain app or a bad habit, take the step in the habit development section in order to cultivate a better habit.

Increasing Your Mental Energy

Use your energy skillfully

Stop working and focus on your breath for a while. Slow down and reflect on your goals, to create an easier path for greatness. Do not just stick to one methodology in getting things done; apply different methods as much as you have access to.

Keep your energy in control and never go beyond your physical or mental capability. Always focus on what you know how to do best and find different ways of doing them. Allow for more breaks during the work process by making sure you stop from time to time. After spending weeks working on a project, you are free to take a complete week break to make sure you reenergize.

Use every possibility

Do not limit yourself to the information you can access during a work process. Also, keep track of the ideas that usually come to mind during breaks. Take the chance to reflect back on your baby ideas and relate them to the present day. Thus you can purge your creative mind and as a result discover a pathway to a particular breakthrough.

Be compassionate to strangers

Becoming instantly compassionate with strangers will help us to leverage our creative energy unto something productive instead of wasting it away on being defensive. New ideas and perspectives can be discovered and you won't need to look anywhere else.

Become nice to strangers without any concrete reason in order to motivate your mental discipline for emotional intelligence. This will also make sure you have control of the situation by becoming nice instead of ignoring them in their times of needs.

When someone exerts negative energy, try as much as possible to think about logical reasons behind their behavior before reacting. Always try to understand individual's perception in order to exercise self-discipline in the public.

Manage strong emotions

The mental coordination is directly affected by the kind of emotions that drives a person. You should focus on the common emotions that may reduce your mental organization. Such emotions include jealousy, hatred, sadness, anger and overexcitement.

Composure is the basic element for mental coordination, and for the creative mind to function at its best. Do not make the mistake of relieving your frustrations on the people closest to you. Always find a way to keep emotional break-downs within. Do not make decisions when you are angry or overexcited.

Get active

Do not ignore the power of physical exercises in boosting mental energy. According to a recent research, a 7 minutes daily exercise is enough to keep the brain stimulated and lubricated to solve insightful problems. Focus on physical exercises every morning, even if it means jogging around the block.

If you can't perform physical exercises in the morning, resort to evening exercises. Remember these short exercises should be intensive due to the small time range needed. So, instead of jogging slowly for 30 minutes, you can double your speed and just run for 7 minutes.

Conclusion

Develop a proper self-awareness about your routine, your energy level and your ability to keep up with new activities. Mindful living is the core of every self-improvement exercise. Self-discipline can be learned and implemented in every situation only when you are fully aware of the benefits and usefulness in respect to the particular situation.

You should continuously make time to understand the causes of your lack of self-discipline and also pinpoint the problems accompanying any relapse. Always know your motivations and your weaknesses. Whenever you encounter a fluctuation in your dedication to your work or passion, find out the reasons and the potentials for creating a permanent change.

Always involve people in your quest for self-discipline, people with similar aims and objectives. Use them as a source of motivation and as a reminder to do even better. From time to time, arrange a personal consultation with a smart person. Stimulate your mind to keep up with the standards of the person in order to seek for clarity on your level of discernment. Recover from mistakes effectively and always focus on long-term results of your self-discipline.